THE GHOSTLY TALES OF ARIZONA'S HAUNTED ROUTE 66

Published by Arcadia Children's Books
A Division of Arcadia Publishing, Inc.
Charleston, SC
www.arcadiapublishing.com

First published 2024
Manufactured in the United States

Designed by Jessica Nevins
Images used courtesy of Shutterstock.com; p. 6 Lost_in_the_MidwestShutterstock.com; p. 12 DCA88Shutterstock.com; p. 18 CaseyMartin/Shutterstock.com; p. 24 nick clephane/Shutterstock.com; p. 30 Debe Branning; p. 38 Logan BushShutterstock.com; p. 46 Marine 69-71/File:Two Guns-Apache Death Cave-.jpg/Wikimedia Commons/CC BY-SA 4.0; pp. 58, 66 Fotoluminate LLC/Shutterstock.com; p. 72 Bob Hilscher/Shutterstock.com; p. 86 Steve Lagreca/Shutterstock.com; p. 92 Upstateherd/File:Brunswick Hotel.jpg/Wikimedia Commons/CC BY-SA 4.0; p. 96 Greta Gabaglio/Shutterstock.com; p. 102 Jon Chica/Shutterstock.com.

ISBN: 9781467197793
Library of Congress Control Number: 2024939039

Spooky America

THE GHOSTLY TALES OF ARIZONA'S HAUNTED ROUTE 66

DEBE BRANNING

Adapted from *Arizona's Haunted Route 66* by Debe Branning

UT CO

NM

NV

CA

Route 66

13

14

16 15

12 11 9 8 6 4 1

10 7 5 3 2

Arizona

Table of Contents & Map Key

ROUTE
US
66

Welcome to Arizona's Spooky Route 66!

Every summer, my family would load into our car and head out on the road for a one- or two-week road trip vacation where we would visit historic landmarks, national monuments, and buy silly souvenirs at various trading posts. My mom had a cooler packed with a picnic lunch so we could stop at roadside picnic tables to eat and enjoy a short break before heading back down the highway. My sister and I argued for the special spot in the back seat, and Mom always carried an extra roll of toilet paper in her bag for emergencies. We played license plate bingo and looked for various signs along the roadway. One of the road trips my family took was along Arizona's Route 66.

Route 66 was probably the most sought-out highway for vacationing travelers in the 1940s, 1950s, and 1960s. It consisted of 2,448 miles of blacktop across eight states—from Chicago, Illinois, to the ocean views of Santa Monica, California. In between, travelers explored Missouri, Kansas, Oklahoma, Texas, New Mexico, and Arizona—places most travelers had never dreamed of seeing! The cities and towns offered museums, attractions, cafes with homecooked meals, and cozy places to sleep at night. There were many shops along the way where travelers could buy postcards and trinkets for family and friends.

Sadly, as time passed, the number of road-tripping motorists decreased. Travel was suddenly all about how quickly vacationers could arrive at their next destination. The new Interstate Highway 40 was planned and developed with that goal in mind. By 1984, most of the small towns and businesses were suddenly bypassed and left to become ghost towns along the dusty Arizona desert.

However, some people who traveled Arizona's Route 66 are still there (well, their ghosts are still there), and you just might see them if you happen to be driving along one of the country's most iconic highways.

Many people believe Arizona has the most haunted stretches of old Route 66. So, pack your bags, buckle up, and get ready for some spooky kicks on Route 66!

NATIONAL
PARK
SERVICE
PETRIFIED FOREST
NATIONAL PARK
UNITED STATES DEPARTMENT OF THE INTERIOR
NATIONAL PARK SERVICE

Curse of the Petrified Forest

We'll start our road trip on the eastern end of Arizona's Route 66, near Petrified Forest National Park. However, only traces of the old roadbed and weathered wooden telephone poles mark the original path of the highway through the park. And it's the only park in the National Park System with a section of the iconic highway.

In this park, which lies within the Painted Desert, you can find remains of ancient conifer trees preserved as stone. During the Triassic Age, over 200 million years ago, these enormous trees, up to nine feet in diameter and over 200 feet tall, were uprooted by powerful floods and buried by the silt of the sandy floodplains. Water seeped into the wood and replaced the decaying organic material with multicolored silica. (Silica is a mineral that is like sand.) The lack of oxygen slowed the decay of the wood, allowing the silica to replace cell walls and fill spaces in the wood.

Early explorers of the area in the mid-1800s collected pieces of the wood as keepsakes. As time went on, wagons, trucks, and early autos were loaded with petrified wood relics and hauled away to be sold as souvenirs.

When the Petrified Forest was named a National Monument in 1906, it became illegal to remove any samples of petrified wood. (The Petrified Forest became a National Park in 1962.) Stealing any pieces of the wood can result in large fines. But that has not always stopped tourists and rock collectors from removing a piece of ancient history from the park. Park officials report that over twelve tons of petrified wood is stolen each year!

Visitors believe they can be sneaky and that no one will ever notice just one little rock missing as they toss it in their backpack or pocket while hiking the trails. However, many petrified wood thieves soon learned that taking the treasure home wasn't such a good idea after all.

In the 1930s, Route 66 visitors to the Petrified Forest began to send in written letters stating that after taking *one* piece of petrified wood from the park, they were suddenly blasted with lots of bad luck. There's a display in a room at the Rainbow Forest Museum at the Petrified Forest National Park dedicated to the hundreds of "cursed thieves" who took just one small rock during their visit. Visitors can read the tear-stained confession letters and emails from thieves stating they encountered car problems during their travels, lost their jobs, had their house burn down, or developed health issues. Some even went to jail! Envelopes, and sometimes *boxes* of stolen rocks, are delivered back to the park on a regular basis.

The park has created an area near the building that the rangers like to call the "Conscience

Rock Pile" where guests can respectfully, and anonymously, return the stolen petrified wood. Guests who think the curse is a hoax can look through the binder containing travelers' letters from all over the world begging for forgiveness. Some of the letters include detailed maps asking the park rangers to please return the artifacts to the exact place from where the petrified wood was stolen.

One of these letters reads, "Believe me... If I would have known the curse went with any of the rocks, I never would have taken these. My life has been *totally destroyed* since we've been back from vacation. Please take these so my life will get back to normal. Let me start over again. Forgive me for ever taking these rocks home."

Tourists are not the only believers in the superstitions and curse. Members of the Navajo Nation do not touch petrified wood because they believe it to be sacred. In Navajo legends, pieces of the petrified wood, or "yei-bits-in," were bones of the greatest and fiercest of all the alien gods—a strong and mighty giant named Yeitso, whom their ancestors killed when they first came to the area.

But never fear! Tourists can purchase petrified wood, which has been collected legally from private land, at several nearby souvenir shops. And thankfully, the curse does not come attached to them . . . or so they say. Keep your fingers crossed!

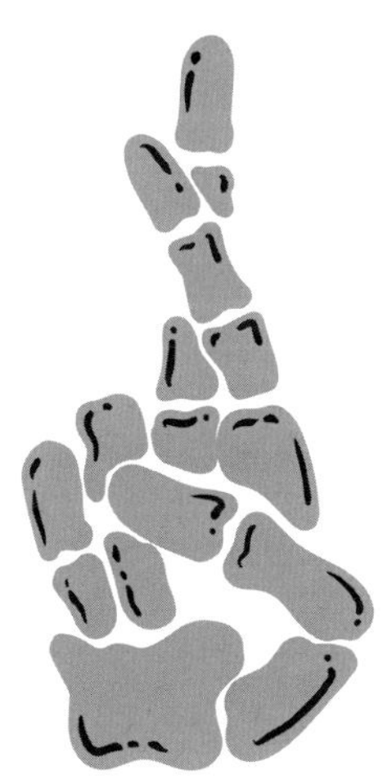

Navajo County Courthouse

The Haunted Navajo County Courthouse

Founded in 1881, Holbrook is about twenty-six miles west of the Petrified Forest National Park along Route 66. And it is still a popular stop along the highway. History shows that Holbrook (the county seat for Navajo County) was once as wild and woolly as Tombstone, Arizona (home of the infamous gunfight at the O.K. Corral), and brags of an equally deadly shootout along one of its streets.

In 1898, Navajo County built a new courthouse that would be the setting for several notorious courtroom trials through the years. The basement of the courthouse housed the sheriff's office and jail cells.

Within a year of the courthouse opening, it played host to one of the most debated hangings of the time. The new courthouse jail was holding a notorious murderer named George Smiley inside its cells. Smiley had been convicted of killing a railroad foreman employee and was sentenced to hang on December 8, 1899.

Back then, Arizona law required that the county sheriff send invitations for executions to all the other Arizona sheriffs. Sheriff Frank Wattron sent a very oddly worded invitation printed on fancy gilt-bordered paper. The invitation ended up in the hands of President William McKinley, who felt the invitation to the hanging was too light-hearted and did not reflect the seriousness of the event. He sent a telegraph to the Arizona territorial governor about the thoughtless invitation and stated that George Smiley's hanging should be delayed for thirty days. The president also issued a stern warning to Wattron for sending the unusual notice of the hanging.

George Smiley was finally hanged on the front courthouse grounds on January 8, 1900. He'd be the first and only man ever hanged in Navajo County. Many employees and visitors to the Navajo County Courthouse say they've seen George Smiley's spirit wandering through the old courthouse and pacing up and down the wooden staircase. The Historical Society Museum staff often blames the noisy ghost for opening and closing doors, heavy footsteps on the second floor, and the strange voices and sounds heard throughout the building. Objects have also mysteriously moved or completely disappeared!

The other courthouse ghost is a woman named Mary. The employees say Mary hanged herself in one of the women's jail cells. A former tourism director and his family were driving past the courthouse one evening and noticed some lights on in the building. He parked the car and went inside the empty courthouse to turn them off. While inside, his wife noticed a woman looking out one of the second-floor windows. She ran inside to alert her husband. Together, the couple searched the entire two-story courthouse but didn't find anyone inside. They're not the only people to witness the ghost of Mary. Many courthouse visitors claim to have seen a mysterious woman peering out an upstairs window. Is Mary's ghost hoping to find freedom?

Cindy Lee and Debe Branning of the MVD Ghostchasers visited the Navajo County Courthouse in 2009 to learn more about its mysterious ghosts. The tour guide at the desk informed them about the building's history and shared a few ghost stories of his own. He talked about a team of paranormal investigators who visited the museum in December 2008. Three psychics with the investigators felt the presence of several spirits in the building. Besides George Smiley and Mary, they sensed that the ghost of Sheriff Frank Wattron is also still on the job! The psychics stated they were able to channel the spirit of Mary in a room on the second floor. That was the first place Cindy and Debe decided to visit!

Upstairs, they found a small room used to house women when the jail cells were full. They placed an EMF (electromagnetic field) meter on the bed.

(Ghost hunters use EMF meters to detect changes in an electromagnetic environment believed to be caused by paranormal activity.). Debe put her purse down on a wooden chair and placed a digital recorder beside it. They began to ask the spirit of Mary several questions. Out of the corner of her eye, Debe thought she saw the fringe on her purse slowly move. Then Debe and Cindy heard what sounded like faint footsteps enter the room. They stood very quietly, waiting to see what might happen next. Suddenly, they saw the fringe on the purse flip into the air as if someone was running their fingers through it.

The tour guide was not sure why Sheriff Frank Wattron would still be haunting the old jail cells. Debe explained that sometimes the dead come back to visit the places that were special to them. Wattron may still believe he is a protector of the law and order within the courthouse. Debe noted that Wattron and Smiley probably do not even "see" each other during their ghostly visits to the building . . . but are still doing time along Route 66.

Wigwam Village Motel

Elvis and the Wigwam Village Motel

The Wigwam Village Motel in Holbrook provides Route 66 travelers a unique and fun opportunity to "sleep in a Wigwam," just like many families did in the heyday of Route 66 travel in the 1950s, '60s, and '70s. Arizona motel owner, Chester E. Lewis, constructed the Wigwam Village in 1950. Its location is full of Old West history and holds stories of many superstitions. There are only fifteen wigwams at the motel, but they're numbered through sixteen because, as always, number *thirteen* is traditionally an unlucky number! And guess what: your motel stay may even come with a very famous ghost!

Debe Branning was leading her annual road trip event, "The Cemetery Crawl," where folks traveled across Arizona to historic attractions and cemeteries learning interesting tales. While checking the teams into the famed Wigwam Village Motel, a strange man strolled into the lobby and

looked around the room. Oddly, he happened to look a lot like the famous rock 'n' roll star, Elvis Presley!

The man posed for photos and quietly retreated to his teepee in the circle of Wigwams. His vehicle was parked out front with a personalized license plate that read *ELVIS,* of course! The group of road trippers joked how they always seem to run into *Elvis* in some shape or form. Sometimes it was a statue, restaurant name, a room named for him, or another silly gimmick—but never in person!

The group went out to dinner at a local Route 66 diner and came back about 9:00 p.m. to prepare for a good night's sleep. At about 9:45 p.m., however, the neon lights in the motel parking lot flipped

on to showcase their bright colors. The sound of Native American drumming filled the quiet circle of teepees. Debe believed it was a "lights out" tradition the motel presented each evening before bedtime. The drums pounded louder and louder. Curious, Debe slowly opened her wigwam door. There, in the middle of the parking lot, stood Elvis holding a bright lantern and a boom box over his head blasting the drums and flute music.

"Just thought I'd have a little fun!" he said, smiling, in that famous Elvis drawl. "Goodnight, hon!"

Startled, Debe quickly shut the door. She couldn't quite put her finger on it, but something about the man suddenly felt very eerie! Her arms broke out in goosebumps, just like they did whenever a paranormal presence was near. Her pulse quickened. Could this man actually be . . . a *ghost*? But not just ANY ghost.

"Who was that?" asked Kenton Moore.

"Why, the *ghost of Elvis*, of course!" Debe exclaimed, before giving him a thumbs up.

The next morning, the teams were up early.

They enjoyed a quick breakfast before continuing back toward Phoenix. There was no sign of Elvis, nor the vehicle whose license plate bore his name. The man had vanished without a trace—as if he had never been at the motel at all.

What do you think? Is the ghost of Elvis reliving the best days of his life, traveling up and down the highway of old Route 66 for all eternity?

The WINSLOW THEATER

The Spooky Starlet of the Winslow Theater

About thirty miles down the road from Holbrook is Winslow, home of the historic Rialto Theater, now known as the Winslow Theatre. The grand Rialto Theater opened its doors in July 1927. The new theater had fine opera chairs and an air conditioning system, which was unusual for the time. It was said to be one of the finest theaters in northern Arizona. When it first opened, the theater featured live stage acts, but it later became a movie house. The theater offered silent movies until 1929, when a $20,000 sound system was installed to welcome the arrival of "talkies" (movies with sound).

A major fire damaged the theater in 1953, but the building was quickly renovated. The theater suddenly closed in 1996 and sat boarded up for many years, but it has recently reopened and is once again showing movies to the delight of local moviegoers

Several theater goers say a ghost of a man sits in the same seat in the theater, as though he's still watching a favorite movie on the screen. After entering the theater, he takes a seat down in front near the lower left-hand side of the stage and watches matinees from another time.

Various managers have lived in an apartment above

the theater. They claim to have felt the presence of someone moving around in their living quarters. One couple saw a watermelon roll along the floor, cross the room, and then suddenly stop! To their amazement, it rolled back to where it originally came from.

It's claimed that the theater has a bit of an unpleasant past. According to legend, an actress named Rose died by suicide in the theater in the 1930s. Apparently, the actor she was madly in love with did not return her romantic feelings, so she sadly ended her life.

The MVD Ghostchasers paranormal investigation crew was given permission to explore the theater basement on a stormy evening in July 2006. There's a set of stairs that leads to the spooky catacombs under the theater backstage, behind the movie screen. The paranormal investigators explored several small dressing rooms from the old vaudeville days. One of these rooms was said to belong to Rose. Staff described how Rose's sweet perfume still floats in the air near the vicinity of her dressing room. Rose did not disappoint the ghost hunters. For a short time, the fragrance of sweet roses filled the hallway near her room.

Angela Archibeque is the owner of nearby Earl's Route 66 Motor Court. She told the Route 66 researchers that while visiting friends who managed the theater, she looked in the auditorium and saw the ghost of Rose walking in the aisle holding the hands of two little spirit girls.

Although it startled Angela to see the ghosts, the three spirits seemed peaceful and caused no harm.

We have found no records of an actress named Rose in the Winslow newspapers. Could theater goers be confusing the story with the passing of local actress, Leorena Shipley, who drowned in a nearby creek? Or could the energy be Mary, the faithful movie goer who suffered a fatal heart attack while watching a matinee at the Rialto Theater in 1959. Although we can't be sure of who the Winslow Theater ghosts are, make sure you save them a seat if you decide to take in a movie there.

Tunnel below Bojo's Grill & Sports Club

Bojo's Hidden Ghostly Tunnels

Bruchman's Trading Post opened in the early 1920s among the busy shops on Winslow's Second Street. In the beginning, the trading post served the Navajo who bought and traded goods there. The popular trading post was run by Robert M. Bruchman, and he and his family resided in an apartment above the business. R. M. Bruchman respected the Navajo and loved learning about their lives, lore, and traditions.

Winslow residents admired Mr. Bruchman and agreed he was a fine gentleman and good businessman. Bruchman often smoked cigars as he worked in his office late at night, taking inventory and doing audits.

Eventually, the Navajo bought vehicles and began shopping at local supermarkets and department stores. The need for a trading post began to decline. But when Route 66 was built, Bruchman's Trading Post happened to be located on the popular highway, and it became a stopping point for tourists who came to buy souvenirs and Navajo crafts and art. In fact, author Debe Branning remembers stopping there in the mid-1970s to purchase a turquoise Mickey Mouse ring! Bruchman's Trading Post closed for good in 1995.

The building now houses the popular BoJo's Grill & Sports Club. In July 2006, the MVD Ghostchasers led a paranormal workshop at the La Posada Hotel, which is a few blocks east of BoJo's Grill and Sports Club. The hungry group of ghost hunters decided to walk to BoJo's for dinner before their evening of paranormal investigations. They filled the restaurant's entire dining area, and some of the group opted to sit in the adjoining sports section.

They begged the wait staff to share their first-hand ghost experiences. The servers offered personal tales of unexplained encounters with Mr. Bruchman's ghost, who they feel still oversees the activities in the building.

"We call him Grandpa," a waitress giggled. "He just gives you that warm feeling of a kind old man—like somebody's grandpa."

"And sometimes, we still smell his cigar smoke," another waiter added. "We can always tell when he's around because we smell the tobacco of a fine cigar."

The kitchen staff reported hearing noises, as if someone is puttering around in the kitchen. Pots and pans get moved or tossed about the kitchen preparation area. The cooks have heard their names called out or whispered in their ear.

One waiter mentioned a secret door in the kitchen that lead to underground tunnels—sweet music to any ghost hunter's ears! The small group in the dining room listened closely as he told them about the system of tunnels running under the city of Winslow that Chinese railroad workers used.

In the late 1800s, Chinese workers helped build the Transcontinental Railroad that connected the East Coast and West Coast of the United States. In many Arizona railroad towns, the Chinese built tunnels so they had a way of traveling through neighborhoods without showing themselves on the streets after dark. (The Chinese suffered discrimination and were treated unjustly because of their race.) The waiter pointed to a sealed trapdoor near the counter, which was likely used in earlier days to move trading post items to a storage area below.

One of the ghost hunters volunteered to go down into the tunnels to take a few pictures and search for any paranormal activity waiting below. He was led into the kitchen, where a staff member opened a locked door with his key. After climbing down a set of rickety wooden steps, the hunter found himself in the cold, dark basement. Armed with only a small flashlight, the ghost hunter made his way by taking pictures as he wandered through the pitch-black tunnel. He soon became a little nervous and turned around, fearing he might go too far and not find his way back to BoJo's kitchen.

In 2020, a group of Route 66 paranormal investigators decided to have dinner at BoJo's during their research trip. Debe Branning recapped the story of the 2006 encounter with its underground tunnels. "There was a trapdoor in the other room, but it looks like they've retiled the floor and covered it up."

Debe walked over to the adjoining room but saw no signs of the trapdoor. She decided to ask their waitress, but the waitress had no clue about any trapdoor or mysterious underground tunnels. The baffled food server called the current owner to verify. To her surprise, he knew all about the tunnels! The stunned waitress passed the phone over to Debe, and the owner invited the group to take the kitchen passageway to the basement and witness the old tunnels themselves. An unplanned paranormal investigation was underway!

When the rickety boards along the basement pathway began to get a bit shaky, Chance Houston, Colleen Sulzer, and Fallon Franzen continued into the next passageway alone.

"Keep looking up!" Debe shouted to them as she snapped more photos. "Look for the trapdoor!"

And sure enough—they hit the jackpot!

"We found it!" Chance yelled from the adjoining room. "It's really here! You were right!"

The next time you are dining at BoJo's, be on the lookout for the spirit of Mr. Bruchman still working late in the evening at his former trading post. A hint of his cigar smoke may still linger in the air and you might hear footsteps coming from the old living quarters above the café—you might even hear your name whispered softly in your ear!

Abandoned Zoo on Route 66

The Ghoulish Desert Zoo Grounds

As you continue west on Route 66, keep your eyes open for the ghost town of Two Guns. This easy-to-miss spot silently sits just south of the busy freeway, about twenty-five miles west of Winslow. Although it's now fading into history, it was a very popular tourist attraction from the 1930s to the 1960s.

The town was originally called Canyon Lodge because of its location near the notorious Diablo Canyon. This deep and scary canyon was once known to be a tough obstacle for travelers going west. The name the Spaniards gave it was a big clue—"Canyon Diablo," which means "Devil's Canyon"—though some say the name really came from Native American legends about the canyon being cursed. Maybe the legends were true.

When the road running through the town was later renamed Route 66, the town's name was changed as well. It's said the small tourist center was renamed Two Guns after a local resident called "Two Guns Miller."

Two Guns flourished in the 1940s. The tourist stop along busy Route 66 included a gas station, café, souvenir shop, and lodgings for an overnight stay. Later, a desert zoo was added to the complex that included almost every mammal and bird native to Arizona. Mountain lions, panthers, and

bobcats were housed in cages that clung to the north side of the canyon wall.

When Interstate 40 was built, it bypassed Two Guns, and the town's popularity began to fade. The fast, non-stop flow of traffic on the new superhighway kept visitors away. Although there were attempts to revive the town, it still sits abandoned and lonely to this day. The ruins of the town and the zoo sit quietly near the old Route 66 Highway Bridge that crosses Canyon Diablo.

Nikki Wheeler, Shiela McCurdy, and Debe Branning of MVD Ghostchasers decided to explore Two Guns on a hot July summer day in 2004. First, they followed a dirt road that led to a long-forgotten Route 66 bridge. They stopped to examine the condition of the structure. There were

gaps on each side of the bridge where safety rails were missing. The bridge seemed very narrow by today's standards. Everyone held their breath as the truck slowly inched along the old concrete.

Once across the bridge, they continued driving toward the abandoned wildlife zoo. A hiker was returning to his vehicle to get a bottle of water. While Shiela and Nikki wandered down an old narrow trail, Debe paused to chat with the gentleman about the history of Two Guns. He told Debe everything he knew about Two Guns and Canyon Diablo.

In 1921, Earle and Louise Cundiff purchased a little over 300 acres of land and constructed a large stone building on the west side of the canyon. The following year, they built a restaurant and installed gas pumps.

Harry "Indian" Miller, who called himself Chief Crazy Thunder, came along in 1926. He leased a portion of the land and opened a trading post and small wildlife zoo.

On March 3, 1926, Miller faced serious charges when he was accused of murdering Earl M. Cundiff at Canyon Lodge. Cundiff was postmaster as well as proprietor of the store. His wife reported there had been an argument between the two men concerning goods, which Cundiff claimed Miller had stolen from his store. Miller insisted that Cundiff threatened him with a revolver, and in wrestling the weapon from Cundiff, it discharged, wounding Cundiff. Miller then shot Cundiff twice in self-defense, the wounds proving fatal. The jury found Miller not guilty.

Perhaps they should have listened to the Native American warnings. The eerie land where Two Guns lies could be cursed! The bad luck did not end there. Miller lost a legal battle with Cundiff's widow over property rights in 1930. Some say his store even burned to the ground. Eventually, after

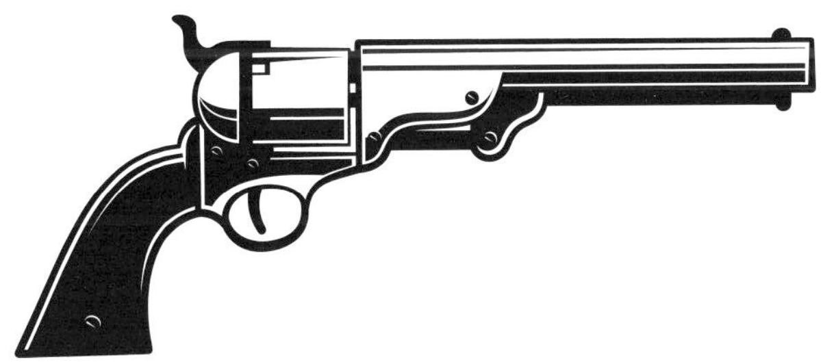

much misfortune, he was forced to pack up and move on. Harry "Indian" Miller headed east where he attempted to set up a similar zoo at a trading post along Route 66 in Lupton, Arizona. He died in New Mexico in 1952.

The curse seemed to continue when in 1938, Route 66 was rerouted to the opposite side of the canyon. Louise Cundiff and her new husband were forced to rebuild everything, including the zoo on the other side, a few yards away. It was sold in the 1950s with the rest of the property, but it seemed nobody could keep the place open for long.

In the 1960s, Ben Dreher built a new motel, café, and gift shop, and reopened the zoo. For a while, it looked like Two Guns might come alive again. But unfortunately, the supposed curse seemed to step in once more. In 1971, Dreher's hard work went up in flames, destroying his dreams of keeping the attraction open.

After the hiker finished telling the story of Two Guns, he and Debe shook hands. He climbed into his truck and drove away, leaving the women to explore what was left of the old gas station and souvenir shop. The desert winds blew eerie whispers past their ears, confirming the tragic and fateful events that took place in this spot.

Today, it's still a place filled with supernatural energy and amazing Arizona history. If you happen to visit Two Guns on your own road trip west down Route 66, perhaps you *too* will feel the strange energy that still lingers there after all these years . . .

Apache Death Cave

Spirits of the Apache Death Cave

On the south side of Two Guns, not far from Canyon Diablo, is the Apache Death Cave. It was the site of an infamous attack on the Apache by their Navajo enemies in 1878. Because of its bloody history and what may remain belowground, the Apache Death Cave is one of the most haunted locations along Route 66. The cave is actually a series of natural caverns that extend for several miles under the brown sandstone.

During the 1870s, the Apache in the area conducted raids on Navajo villages and disappeared into the desert before they could be tracked down. This went on for almost a decade. In the summer of 1878, the Apache attacked a Navajo settlement, killing nearly every Navajo man, woman, and child. When the Apache finished looting the encampment, only three girls remained, and the Apache took them prisoner.

When the Navajo leaders learned of this attack, they sent a scouting party to track the Apache across the desert. Their efforts failed as, once again, the Apache raiders slipped away. But eventually, a group of Navajo scouts noticed warm air, the smell of cooking fires, and voices rising from a crevice in the ground. They had discovered the underground cave where the Apache were hiding. The cave was large enough to house the raiding party, their horses, and the stolen goods. The Navajo located the mouth of the cave in a rocky ravine. They dropped wood and sagebrush at the entrance of the ravine and lit it on fire!

With smoke flowing into the cave entrance, the Apaches were trapped! Those who dared to try and escape were found by the waiting Navajo warriors.

The Apache used what little water they had to douse the fire, but it wasn't enough. With the Navajo continuing to feed the fire, they realized they were doomed. Smoke rose from the crack in the rocks that the Navajo had discovered, carrying the voices of the Apache as they sang death chants.

When the songs faded and the smoke began to clear, the Navajo discovered the bodies of forty-two Apache warriors and their horses. They retrieved their stolen goods and valuables and quickly rode away in triumph.

According to legend, that was the last time the Apache set foot in the cave, and they never

again raided the Navajo people. Many tribes have since avoided the cave, considering it and the surrounding land to be cursed!

Local tribes tried to warn would-be settlers about the cave, insisting the land around it was haunted. Settlers often passed this off as silly superstition, but those who made their home on the land reported hearing ghostly groans and footsteps outside their rustic cabins.

Hiking down to the Apache Cave was high on the priority list for the Route 66 paranormal investigators. Armed with recording devices, cameras, and walking sticks to fight off rattle snakes and bats, the group parked nearby and hiked up to the edge of the cliff that overlooked the cave entrance.

Even with the constant background noise of Interstate 40 just north of the section of old Route 66, it was still a good place to pause and feel the energy of the spirits who met their fate there. Most paranormal investigators and visitors to Apache Death Cave say it feels otherworldly. Whether or not you believe in ghosts, it is hard to deny the eerie energy that draws you in and surrounds you when you step foot there.

One of the ghostchasers reflected, "I physically heard and felt the emotional pain and fear. The closer I came to the entrance, the harder it was to breathe and the quieter it got."

Fact or legend, the Apache Death Cave is a very spiritual site. Though the scariest part nowadays may be rattlesnakes and bats, brave visitors who enter the cave report uneasy feelings.

Fear. Pain. Sadness. Grief.

Could it be their imaginations running away with them?

Or could it be the spirits of the forty-two Apache . . . trapped for all eternity?

Riordan Mansion

The Relatively Haunted Riordan Mansion

Our next stop is Flagstaff, about forty miles west of Two Guns. It's home to the historic Riordan Mansion, built in 1904 by lumber baron brothers Timothy and Michael Riordan. The brothers married two sisters, Caroline and Elizabeth Metz, and the mansion was home to both their families. It consisted of two large and luxurious wings, one for each family, connected by a billiard room.

The Riordan brothers, who owned the Arizona Lumber and Timber Company, built their 13,000-square-foot mansion while Arizona was still a territory struggling to gain statehood. It is one of Arizona's most historic and elegant pioneer homes.

The two couples raised their families in their private quarters, but each evening, the families would gather for activities in the large billiard room in the center of the living complex. The Riordan's joined together in song, prayer, games, and other forms of entertainment. At the end of the day, the families would retire to their separate living area.

Visitors say the energy in the billiard room can be overwhelming. Arthur, the oldest son of Michael and Elizabeth, had his own encounter with the supernatural as a young man when staying in the house all alone. The two families had gone off on a special outing that day, but Arthur was not feeling well and had decided to stay home. He was upstairs in his room when, suddenly, he heard the pool balls clicking on the billiard table. Thinking perhaps another family member had returned home, he ran to investigate. But when he got downstairs . . . nobody was there.

Arthur shrugged and went back upstairs to his room. A short time later, however, the ghostly pool game started up again. This time when Arthur hurried down the stairs, he witnessed the balls moving across the table. Once again, there was nobody in the billiard room except him.

The billiard room has also witnessed some tragedies. On September 8, 1927, Michael's son, Arthur, and Timothy's youngest daughter, Anna, died within hours of each other from the complications of polio. Since the disease was contagious, the Riordans held the joint funeral in the billiard room. The two families and the priest were the only mourners in attendance.

The family was very religious and had a small chapel on the second floor of the home. A local legend says that the Riordans always kept a light burning in the chapel. It mysteriously burned out the moment of Caroline's death in 1943.

Riordan Mansion is now part of the Arizona State Park system, and many areas of the home are open for guided tours. Although the building is not said to be haunted, the staff will admit there have been some "strange happenings" from time to time. Occasionally, guests will connect with a guide who has witnessed paranormal activity on a tour or while doing maintenance work in the mansion. Debe Branning once joined an afternoon guided tour, and the guide had several ghostly tales to tell the interested group.

She told them about the ghost of Caroline Riordan, who is known to walk the hallways in search of her daughter Anna. Only twenty-six at the time of her death and soon to be married, her life was taken by a sudden illness. To this day, Anna's photo and college commencement announcement still decorate the wall of the small bedroom.

The tour guide pointed out a painting of Timothy's oldest daughter, Mary, which hangs in the living room over the fireplace. As you walk around the room, be sure to notice how her head and torso appear to turn and follow you. A mere optical illusion? Or . . . could the painting itself be touched with the supernatural? While you're in Flagstaff, why not visit the spooky Riordan Mansion and find out for yourself?

HOTEL
MONTE VIST
ASPEN AVE
ONE WAY
ONE WAY

Spirited Stars at Hotel Monte Vista

Thanks to the growing popularity of the automobile in the 1920s, the number of visitors to Flagstaff significantly increased during that time. Residents decided they needed a first-class hotel to accommodate the many travelers making their way along Route 66. The money to build the hotel was raised by donations from prominent citizens and Zane Gray, a famous author who lived in Flagstaff at the time.

Sitting at the corner of Aspen and San Francisco

Streets, the hotel opened on January 1, 1927. It was a full-service hotel and bragged of its running water, flushable toilets, telephones, and room service. Originally called the Community Hotel to honor the people who had helped raise the money to build it, the name was later changed to Hotel Monte Vista. A twelve-year-old contest winner chose the name.

Many Hollywood movie stars filming around the Flagstaff area have been guests of the Monte Vista, and some of the rooms have been named after those celebrity guests. The list includes Humphrey Bogart, Bing Crosby, Debbie Reynolds, John Wayne, Spencer Tracy, Clark Gable, Carole Lombard, Bob Hope, Esther Williams, Michael J. Fox, Jon Bon Jovi, Freddy Mercury, and Freddie Kruger himself—Robert Englund.

Hotel Monte Vista is listed on the National Register of Historic Places, and ghostly guests have been taking extended "staycations" in many of the rooms. The Monte Vista has several ghost stories, but a favorite tale is from a personal experience that paranormal investigator Megan Taylor had during her visit to the landmark hotel.

Megan was snapping pictures as she walked along the third-floor hallway. Suddenly, she saw a man walking toward her down the hall. She didn't want to seem rude and quickly stopped taking pictures. The man walked up to the door of one of the rooms and began to go through the motions of unlocking the door with his key.

Megan said the gentleman looked as real as you or me. But instead of opening the door, the man walked right through it! Megan said the ghost had a strange resemblance to Alan Ladd, an actor famous for his roles in Westerns in the 1940s and 1950s. And the room he entered was Room 309, which happened to be the Alan Ladd room at Hotel Monte Vista!

One of the most famous hauntings involves Room 305—the Bon Jovi room. Some guests have reported seeing an elderly woman

sitting in a rocking chair near the window. Other guests have witnessed the chair rocking on its own or moving to another spot. Nobody knows for sure if someone died in the room, but some investigators speculate it could be the room where Marian Behn lived and died on the third floor. Her daughter, Ruth, worked at the Babbitt department store across the street. The third-story window was the perfect vantage point to keep her motherly eyes upon her daughter.

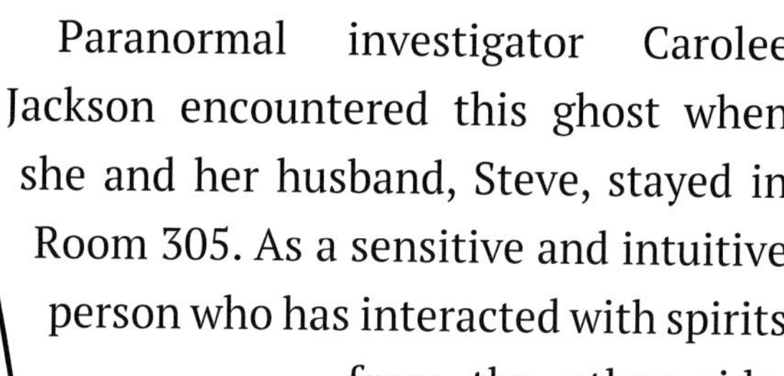

Paranormal investigator Carolee Jackson encountered this ghost when she and her husband, Steve, stayed in Room 305. As a sensitive and intuitive person who has interacted with spirits from the other side, Carolee was anxious for her husband to have first-hand experiences like she has had her entire life. They were not disappointed.

"The first thing we did after unpacking our bags was to use the EMF detector for base readings. The room was quiet except in one area near the bathroom by the window curtains. After dinner we retired to the room for the night. Steve used the EMF detector to recheck the base readings and got nothing—not even where we'd gotten them before?

"I started an EVP (electronic voice phenomena) session with the recorder, and it wasn't long before I had somebody come *through* me and use my energy. At that point, I took the EMF detector in hand and its lights went on. Our visitor was using my energy to contact us. Though shy and wanting to stay by the window curtain, the visitor did give some responses to questions. Those answers were recorded and can be heard in playback."

Carolee knew the visitor was an older woman who had died from heart failure. Before they went to sleep, Carolee moved the rocking chair a couple of inches from where it usually sat.

"There are worn grooves in the carpet, and I moved the chair to the left of those grooves," she stated. "When we woke in the morning, the rocking chair was back in place in the grooves."

Another popular ghost in the hotel is the "phantom bellboy" who knocks on the door of Room 210 and announces, "room service." When guests open the door, nobody is there! It's said that actor John Wayne saw the ghostly bellboy on several occasions. He reported that the ghost seemed friendly, and he didn't feel threatened when it visited him.

There is a long history of spooky deaths in the hotel—not unusual for long-term tenants, travelers, and salesman of the day. This includes a gentleman who perished in the hotel lobby on New Year's Day 1951 while listening to the Rose Bowl game, giving a whole new meaning to a *sudden death* finish. If you decide to book a room, perhaps you'll be visited by one or more of the Monte Vista's ghostly guests. But when you check in, be warned: some guests like it here so much . . . they *never* leave!

ORPHEUM
10/19 PETER ROWAN
21 SEVENDUST
22 FMFF TREKKING & TRAVEL FILM
ORPHEUM BOX OFFICE OPEN MON-SAT
ORPHEUM
ACK BAR
ATM
SLICES

Odd Happenings at the Orpheum Theater

The Orpheum Theater in Flagstaff was built by John Weatherford, who also owned the striking Weatherford Hotel just up the street. Opened in 1911 and originally named the Majestic Opera House, the theater was very popular with the locals and featured a stage, movie screen, and a hardwood dance floor. Sadly, a tragedy occurred on New Year's Eve 1915, nearly putting an end to the movie palace. After the New Year's celebration ended, the roof and walls of the theater collapsed under the weight of five feet of snow. Weatherford was able to save the projector from the theater ruins, and he continued to show movies from a temporary location.

John Weatherford eventually rebuilt his movie house and renamed it the Orpheum. It was bigger and better and served the Flagstaff community from August 1917 until it closed in 1999. For several years, the theater fell silent. But a new owner was found, and the Orpheum reopened in 2002. Today, it continues to serve Flagstaff residents as

northern Arizona's premier performing arts venue.

Many people in Flagstaff say the Orpheum Theater is haunted. A custodian reported seeing a shadowy figure walking up in the balcony late one night. The theater was closed at the time and no one else was in the building. The custodian watched as the dark figure glided back and forth through the aisles of the balcony. The curious worker climbed the stairs to the balcony area to investigate and confirmed there was no one up there. Who or what was this mysterious specter?

One night, the snack counter employees observed a playful ghost in the lobby as the last performance of the night was playing in the theater. A roll of paper towels hanging on a wall dispenser began to unravel onto the concession floor. One worker was brave enough to stop it, but as soon as he let go, the paper towels started to unroll at a faster pace.

Employees and theater guests report hearing unexplained footsteps walking across the lobby floor and unusual phenomena in the men's restroom. One night, after the theater was closed, the after-hours cleaning crew heard all the toilets flushing, and the sinks started running at full blast. Was this a plumbing problem—or was this the prankster ghost?

Theater employees cannot be sure of the ghost's identity. They did point out a tiny crawlspace near the projection room at the very top of the balcony. A ladder leads to the roof and the theater marquee sign. Legend states that a man died by suicide there long ago, but no evidence has been found to support this rumor.

Grab some Milk Duds, popcorn, a drink, and take your seat up in the theater balcony. Just remember that the person wearing that distracting baseball cap in front of you may not be real at all!

The
ROUTE
66
Place
TWISTERS
50's Soda
Fountain
EAT HERE

Twisted Tales of Twisters

About thirty-three miles west of Flagstaff is the town of Williams, home to the Dara Thai Twisters restaurant. The building used to house Twisters Soda Fountain and started out as a busy Texaco Gas Station and repair garage. Vacationers traveling along Route 66 frequently stopped in to get gas at the full-service station. Just about the same time Williams and Route 66 were bypassed by Interstate 40 in the 1980s, the era of full-service gas stations came to an end, too. The welcoming bell that called a full-service gas station attendant to your car went silent.

The most fascinating ghost story connected to this space occurred in 2008, after the owners of the former soda fountain renovated the 1950s diner. They installed the most up-to-date surveillance and alarm system so they could monitor the business from home. Nothing ever activated the motion sensor cameras until October 2008. An alert triggered the alarm at 3:01 a.m., and what the owner observed simply baffled him and his employees.

They watched in disbelief as a white cloudy mist gradually transformed into a shadowy human form—slowly walking through a small hallway in a back area of the diner. The owners played the audio/video recording over and over as they tried to come up with a reasonable explanation. Local TV news channels featured the video as an unsolved ghostly occurrence during the Halloween season. The strange phenomena only happened on that one occasion. It never triggered the alarms inside the diner again.

There have been a few other reports of paranormal activity observed at Twisters in the past. Employees noted that items had fallen off shelves for no reason. One of the owners was balancing the books early one morning when she clearly heard a man inside the building say, "Hello." The voice startled the woman, and she conducted a thorough search of the diner. Much to her relief, there was no intruder. Perhaps it was just the mysterious spirit's way of letting her know he was friendly.

Several paranormal teams in Arizona came to Williams to organize their own investigations at Twisters. The groups monitored the building by setting up night vision cameras—trying to recreate the phenomena captured on film. Some people speculate the ghost could be the former owner of the Texaco Station back in the 1950s. Clial T. Godwin, or "Shorty," as he was known, was rumored to have died by suicide inside the gas station.

Research by Debe Branning confirms Godwin did die by suicide about eighteen miles west of

the town of Seligman, inside his car parked along Route 66. Has Shorty's apparition returned to his former gas station as a misty ghost? Is he staying on the job from the afterlife?

539
KEEP OFF
KEEP OFF

Ghosts of the Fray Marcos Harvey House

In the late 1800s, a businessman named Fred Harvey spent a lot of time traveling by train in the western United States. The roadhouses along the train routes didn't offer very good food or service, and Harvey spotted a business opportunity. He struck a deal with the Atchison, Topeka & Santa Fe Railway to open a chain of restaurants along its rail lines. The first restaurant opened in Topeka, Kansas, in 1876, and Harvey opened his first eatery in Williams when his company took over a local restaurant that had been in service since around 1884.

As part of the staff at his hotels and restaurants, Fred Harvey created the famous Harvey Girls. They are often described as the first all-female workforce. Women came from all over the country to work with the company. The Harvey Girls were known for the excellent service they provided guests, and for the charm and manners they brought to the Wild West. The women were given room and board and wore matching uniforms, which were long black dresses with white aprons. The training was rigorous and there were strict rules.

Architect Francis W. Wilson was selected to design the Harvey company's hotel and restaurant at the new Williams train depot that opened on March 10, 1908. It was named after Spanish Franciscan Missionary Fray Marcos de Niza—the first European explorer of Arizona and New Mexico. The Fray Marcos Hotel offered twenty-two guest rooms and ten dorm rooms for the Harvey Girls when it opened. The rooms had comfortable beds and featured hot and cold running water and bathtubs. The ground floor had a lobby, baggage room, ladies' waiting room, men's waiting room, ticket office, offices, and the famous dining room. The Williams Depot and the original Fray Marcos Hotel are now listed on the National Register of Historic Places.

In the 1920s, the Harvey Company added a two-story addition with twenty-one new guest rooms. Travelers often stayed at the Fray Marcos while enroute to the Grand Canyon by train or car as they traveled along Route 66.

Paranormal investigator Colleen Sulzer explained, "Williams was a rowdy town full of railroad men, cowboys, and workers in lumber mills, so the Fray Marcos was a beautiful sight to see. The refined Harvey Girls were eager to serve this rugged bunch of Arizona pioneers. Historians often praise the Harvey Girls as being a big part of the blazing spirit of the old West."

The Harvey Girl staff of the Fray Marcos lived above the kitchen on the second floor of the west wing. Each small, comfortable room was shared by two Harvey Girls. Their work schedules kept them very busy, and when they were off duty, there were strict chaperones to deal with. On their days off, the girls used railway passes to visit the Grand Canyon and other Arizona cities. They visited friends and traveled the vast open spaces of Northern Arizona in automobiles.

The Harvey Girls at the Fray Marcos always kept the lunchroom counter and dining room tables spotless and ready for the next train arrival. When the staff wasn't serving hungry travelers, they polished the silverware, cleaned the sparkling glasses, and kept the famous Fred Harvey coffee brewing.

Today, the building that housed the Fray Marcos depot restaurant and hotel is the busy Grand Canyon Railway ticket counter, museum, and gift shop. It's still a must-see location for travelers along Route 66 and visitors to the Grand Canyon. Furnishings in the depot and gift shop give a glimpse of what early train travel was like. The fireplace, which was once part of the original lobby and dining area, is still a beautiful feature of the gift shop.

These days, the hotel rooms where tired travelers once slept are used for offices and storage space. Seeing that Fray Marcos was such a favorite place of employment, it's not surprising that some of the Harvey Girl staff would remain at the depot even in the afterlife. According to the current staff, it's believed that one of the Harvey Girls may still be on duty at the old Harvey House. Many of the employees have witnessed her presence.

One of the cashiers noted, "We call the ghost Clara. I haven't seen her myself, but I have felt her presence in the late afternoon or early evening when nobody else is in the shop. You see something move out of the corner of your eye—or hear a movement from the back of the room, and then you just nod and acknowledge Clara. We feel Clara senses we are getting ready to close shop for the night and she's just tidying up the old Harvey House, too."

Other clerks in the gift shop believe mischievous spirits like to play games and rearrange books and souvenir items on shelves or display counters. Cashiers have heard the light clicking of a woman's shoes across the original tile floors as they count out money in the cash drawers. Expecting to see a customer who was left behind or perhaps another employee, they're surprised to discover the train depot completely empty.

An elderly clerk at the Grand Canyon Railway counter saw the spirit of a young woman lingering near the doorway to the dining area. The vision of the smiling ghost lasted a few seconds and faded away. The clerk described the ghost as "resembling a Harvey Girl dressed in a pressed uniform as seen in the museum's photo collection."

Maintenance workers often take a deep breath before going up the staircase to the second floor, where the Grand Canyon Railway offices and cleaning supply storage rooms are located. Startled staff members have seen the black-and-white uniformed ghost of Harvey Girl Clara standing near the top of the second-floor stairs landing. Sometimes, they even refuse to go upstairs alone! They're reminded that the second floor was the old Harvey Girl dormitory where the girls socialized with each other at the end of a long day. Perhaps Clara's ghost is simply dashing downstairs to greet the next breakfast train when she accidentally bumps into the unsuspecting maintenance crew working in *this* realm.

The Grand Canyon Railway staff agree there was once, indeed, a Harvey Girl at the Fray Marcos named Clara in the 1920s and 1930s. Clara's spirit could very well be a dedicated Harvey Girl who loved her job in life and still enjoys waiting on ghostly train travelers in the old Harvey House dining room.

RAND CANYON
CAVERNS
ARIZONA
HISTORIC
ROUTE
66
CURIO SH
OPEN

Ghostly Depths of the Grand Canyon Caverns and Ranch House

About eighty miles west of Williams is the town of Peach Springs, home of the Grand Canyon Caverns. Lucky guests can book the Cavern Suite and sleep 220 feet below ground! However, guests need to be brave as well as lucky, as the caverns are reported to be *very* haunted. Several buildings on the property, including the Ranch House, are sites of some spectacularly spooky ghost tales.

The cavern was discovered by Walter Peck in 1927. The caverns have had many names and owners, including Yampai Caverns, The Coconino

Caverns, and The Dinosaur Caverns before finally being named The Grand Canyon Caverns in 1962. The cavern's entrance is near a Native American sacred burial site, and the caverns are considered a spiritual place. Makeshift ladders, steps, and a swinging bridge were built in the caverns in 1935. An elevator was installed in 1962—and the natural entrance to the cave was eventually sealed.

The inn was constructed in the 1940s. The Ranch House is now used as large family sleeping quarters that can accommodate ten guests.

There has been a ghostly sighting of a man standing inside the elevator. He is seen at either the top or the bottom of the shaft, opening and closing the doors. Cavern employees believe this is the ghost of Walter Peck.

At one time, the ranch house was owned by the Ringsby Trucking Company. Local legend has it that general manager Gary Ringsby died by suicide there in the 1970s. Research showed he died in Colorado and not at the ranch house. However, it appears that Gary still takes his job quite seriously, as his spirit has returned to the place he used to work. Ghost hunters have recorded flickering lights and slamming doors, as well as EMF readings and responses to questions asked of the former general manager.

Strange sounds have been heard near the old wooden staircase close to the Cavern Suite as well as near guests' headboards late at night. Tour guides have experienced walkway chains swinging on their own, small shadows darting near the pathways, and the feeling of being followed. Guides and visitors have reported seeing strange figures, dancing shadows on the rock walls, and hearing chanting.

In February 2013, five paranormal teams met to investigate the caverns and grounds. Using various cameras, meters, and recording devices, the investigators divided into two groups. This gave everyone the opportunity to spend time investigating each location during the night.

The teams took a walking tour with the cavern guide to familiarize themselves with the cave and its surroundings. One investigator, who is not normally sensitive to hauntings, experienced extreme despair near the ladders close to the bridge (old entrance) area of the caverns. The guide had escorted two investigators across the bridge and up in the ladder area to observe the old entrance to the cave. The female investigator began to weep over a "feeling" of someone who had died or had been seriously injured in an accident during construction within the cavern. She believed the name of the injured spirit was "Kevin." It's said the caverns have been the scene of a least eight deaths over the last fifty years.

A third investigator walked about the caverns most of the night. Like the others, he had similar feelings of despair, anguish, and hopelessness near the wooden bridge at the old entrance.

Another investigator saw what she believed to be a young man. She could make out his facial features clearly. He stood just inside the cavern area (near the elevator entrance) looking toward the Cavern Suite. The apparition was just standing there watching. She rushed over to the spot, felt a very cold energy breeze drift past her, and the energy quickly faded away.

The five paranormal teams believe the Grand Canyon Caverns are active due to residual energies that are *imprinted* into the stone walls. Perhaps the mysterious ghosts are not active every night—but watch out for the evenings when haunting spirits do a little caving of their own.

Hotel Brunswick

Hotel Brunswick Specters

About an hour's drive west of Peach Springs is the town of Kingsman, where you'll find The Hotel Brunswick. Built in 1909 by business partners John Mulligan and J.W. Thompson, it was one of the first three-story buildings in the area. In 1912, Mulligan and Thompson got into a fight and literally split the building in half with a wall. Mulligan operated his half as a hotel and bar, while Thompson used his half as a hotel and restaurant. Both sides were very successful, but the two men never spoke to each other again.

The Mulligan family sold the hotel in 1928 and there have been several new owners over the years.

It was no surprise to learn that The Hotel Brunswick is known to be quite haunted. One of the more recent owners reported smelling the scent of lilacs, which she interpreted as being Sarah Mulligan, the wife of John Mulligan. They also heard playful giggles and the scampering of children's footsteps throughout the building. Coins have mysteriously appeared out of nowhere, carefully placed in hidden corners of the hallways and lobby. A male ghost has been seen coming up the rickety cellar steps, and guests report seeing ghostly figures in their rooms. Some guests have even sensed presences that tuck them into bed or touch their heads and feet.

Could one of the ghosts haunting the Brunswick be William D. McCright? Mr. McCright was about seventy-four years old when he was found dead in his room in March 1915. He had moved into the hotel in 1913 and made an appearance at breakfast every morning. When McCright didn't show up one morning, the hotel manager went to his room to check on him. He found McCright lying on the floor, clutching a towel in his hands.

Is he the thoughtful spirit that tucks hotel guests in at night and leaves the coins scattered about the hotel?

Hotel Brunswick is closed until further notice at this time, but perhaps an inspired businessperson will come along and resurrect it, ghosts and all.

El Trovatore
MOTEL
Clean Rooms
FREE HBO & Local Calls
Laundry & Kitchenettes
THEME ROOMS
HISTORIC
Route 66
440
39.99 +TAX
66

Voices of the El Trovatore Motel

The El Trovatore Motel in Kingman is one of the few motels built along Route 66 before World War II that is still in operation. This historic motel started as a service station in 1937, and a motel was added in 1939. Back then, you could get a room for just $3.00 a night. The rooms have a Hollywood theme and honor famous movie-star guests such as Marilyn Monroe, James Dean, and Clark Gable. The motel also has spectacular views of the Hualapai Mountains and Slaughterhouse Canyon.

Legend tells a tale of a pioneer family who lived in Slaughterhouse Canyon. The husband worked in the nearby gold mines and would sometimes be away from the homestead for weeks at a time, earning money to keep his family clothed and fed. One day, the husband waved goodbye to leave for work in the mines, but he never returned. Was he robbed and murdered? Did he become ill? We may never know. His devoted wife and children were left all alone in the canyon with no means of support. Soon, they were all starving, and the children

sobbed and wailed for food. After many days, the mother could not bear to hear her children's painful cries anymore. Tragically, the locals say she killed them and then took her own life.

Some visitors to Slaughterhouse Canyon have spoken of feeling a sadness that fills the air. On moonlit evenings, when the air is very still and thick, locals say you can hear the cries of the hungry children and of the mother in agony who made the tragic decision to end their suffering.

Others have parked in the canyon down by the remains of the old slaughterhouse shack. They roll down the windows and wait quietly for Luana—the name they have given the ghostly mother. They almost always hear strange or eerie noises on the dark, lonely road. Some ghost hunters reported driving down the road that leads into the canyon and seeing a mysterious woman in a black dress and dark veil walking along the road. When they turned around for another look, she had disappeared! Is this ghostly woman the mother of the hungry children, venturing to look for food for her family?

Not long ago, several teams of ghost hunters met up at a diner near the El Trovatore Motel. Talk at the table was about some team members hearing the sounds of children laughing and frolicking in the El Trovatore Motel parking lot around 3:00 a.m.. They later learned that hearing children in the motel's parking lot has been an ongoing phenomenon for many years. These ghostly children have never been seen, but they are often heard by staff and visitors and have become a large part of local lore. Many believe that these children come from the gorge behind the hotel where Indigenous peoples used to live.

If you do happen to stay at the El Trovatore Motel, will you be brave enough to try and make friends with the ghostly children in the parking lot?

Main Street, Oatman

Oatman's "Pearl" of the Mining Town

Our final stop is in Oatman, about a fifty-minute drive west of Kingman. One of the popular attractions in the town is the burros (small wild donkeys) that roam freely through the streets seeking snacks, which the tourists can purchase to feed them. The friendly burros are not corralled at the close of the day. They simply wander back to the nearby hillsides to graze until it is time to return to Oatman to entertain the Route 66 visitors the following day.

The townspeople of Oatman often share the ghostly tale of "Pearl the Burro." The legend states that there once was an old prospector named Howdy. He was rarely seen without his trusty white pack mule, Pearl. Together, the dusty pair was a familiar team in the mining camps. They trusted each other as working partners in the mines for many, many years.

The shopkeepers smiled every time the duo showed up in Oatman to get supplies, water, and food. Howdy did not always have cash in his saddlebag to pay for his purchases, so he often settled his tab by trading a small bag of gold dust for the supplies. Folks say Howdy and Pearl were last seen heading out of town on the north trails that led back up to the mines. It was a dark and stormy evening in late October 1917 when the two of them disappeared into the cold, wet night.

Sadly, a few days later, Pearl was discovered wandering the streets of Oatman all alone. She was running up and down Main Street in a panic, braying loudly and searching for Howdy. Several townsfolk came out of the shops and saloons and tried to calm the grief-stricken burro. Pearl stared at them with pleading eyes and brayed as if to say, "Follow me! Follow me!"

However, no one followed the white burro, so Pearl sadly disappeared back into the darkness of the night all alone. Unfortunately, Howdy was never seen again. Time passed, and strangely, Pearl began to appear on the streets of Oatman whenever there was a full moon. She wandered the streets, braying mournfully to the citizens of Oatman. She was still trying to get them to follow and rescue her partner, Howdy.

Old-timers in Oatman still report that Pearl returns to town whenever there is a full moon. They encourage visitors to snap a photo of her and post it on a bulletin board in the town square. So, if you see a white burro standing on the side of the road, sadly braying in the darkness of night, you might want to ignore what you see. Do not follow the white burro into the hills because it just might be Pearl the ghost burro! And who knows where she might lead you . . .

A Ghostly Goodbye

Route 66 welcomes road trippers with open arms, and just like an old-fashioned road map, you never know what adventures will unfold! There are certainly plenty of ghosts along this historic section of the United States highway system, all willing to share their tales of mystery and tragedy. But are you brave enough to listen? Do you dare to travel with the Ghosts of Arizona's Haunted Route 66? It might be worth hitting the road to find out!

DEBE BRANNING has been the director of the MVD Ghostchasers, a Mesa/Bisbee, AZ-based paranormal team since 1994. The team conducts investigations of haunted, historical locations throughout Arizona and has offered paranormal workshops/investigations since 2002. Debe has been a guest lecturer and speaker at several Arizona universities and community colleges, science fiction and paranormal conferences, historical societies, and libraries.

Her television appearances include an episode of TRAVEL CHANNEL'S "Ghost Stories" about haunted Jerome, Arizona (2010) and an episode of "Ghost Adventures— "Old Gila County Jail and Courthouse" (2018.) As a paranormal journalist, she has investigated haunted locations including castles, jails, ships, inns, cemeteries, and has taken walking ghost tours in the United States, England, Scotland, Ireland, and Mexico. Debe is the author of many spooky books for both children and adults. Visit www.mvdghostchasers.com to learn more!

Check out some of the other *Spooky America* titles available now!

Spooky America was adapted from the creeptastic *Haunted America* series for adults. *Haunted America* explores historical haunts in cities and regions across America. Here's more from the original *Arizona's Haunted Route 66* author, Debe Branning: